The Simile of the Cloth
&
The Discourse on Effacement

Two Discourses of the Buddha
from the Majjhima Nikāya

Edited with Introduction and Notes
by Nyanaponika Thera

BUDDHIST PUBLICATION SOCIETY
Kandy   1988   Sri Lanka.

First published 1964
Second printing 1974
Third printing 1988

Copyright © 1988, Buddhist
  Publication Society

ISBN 955-24-0004-X

Published by
Buddhist Publication Society
P.O. Box 61
54, Sangharaja Mawatha
Kandy, Sri Lanka

Offset in Sri Lanka by
Karunaratne & Sons Ltd.
647, Kularatne Mawatha
Colombo 10

THE WHEEL PUBLICATION NO. 61/62

THE SIMILE OF THE CLOTH

Introduction

This discourse of the Buddha—the seventh in the Collection of Middle Length Texts (Majjhima Nikāya) —deals first with a set of sixteen defilements of the human mind; and in its second part, with the disciple's progress to the highest goal of Arahatship, which can be achieved if—and only if—these impurities are gradually reduced and finally eliminated. While there are also defilements of *insight* which must be removed for the attainment of the goal, the sixteen defilements dealt with here are all of an *ethical* nature and are concerned with man's *social behaviour*. Only the last of these sixteen, negligence, may also refer to purely personal concerns as well as to one's relations with others.

A glance through the list (see Note 2) will show that all these sixteen defilements derive from greediness and selfishness, from aversion, self-assertion and conceit, or their combinations. If we take, for instance, contempt, being a weaker nuance of (5) denigration, we see that aversion and conceit contribute to it; (7) envy is fed by greediness and aversion. The pairs of contributive factors here exemplified do not, of course, occur at the same moment of consciousness; but their repeated, separate presence favours the arising of such derivatives as contempt and envy. On the other hand, if those secondary defilements such as contempt and envy (and all the others) appear frequently, they will bring about a close serial association of their "feeders," as for instance hate motivated by conceit, or hate motivated by greed; and these may easily become habitual sequences, automatic chain-reactions in our impulsive life.

Interlocked in such a manner, the negative forces in our mind—the defilements, roots of evil, and fetters—will become more powerful and much more difficult to dislodge. They will form "closed systems" hard to penetrate, covering ever larger areas of our mind. What may first have been isolated occurrences of unwholesome thoughts and acts, will grow into hardened traits of character productive of an unhappy destiny in future lives (see Discourse Sec. 2). And in all these grave consequences, the secondary or derivative defilements have a great share. Hence it is of vital importance that we do not fall victim to the last in the list of those defilements—negligence—and are not negligent in watchfulness and self-control.

> "Out of regard for your own good, it is proper to strive with heedfulness; out of regard for others' good, it is proper to strive with heedfulness; out of regard for your own and others' good, it is proper to strive with heedfulness."
>
> (Nidāna Saṁy., No. 22)

As to "others' good," how much more pleasant and harmonious will be human relations, individual and communal, if there is less pettiness and peevishness, fewer vanities and jealousies, and less self-assertiveness in words and deeds! As already remarked: if these minor blemishes are reduced, the larger and more serious defilements will have fewer opportunities. How often do deadly conflicts and deep involvement in guilt arise from petty but unresolved resentments!

The composition of our list of defilements alone makes it clear that the Buddha was well aware of the social impact of these impurities; and the structure of the discourse shows that he regarded the removal of these defilements as an integral part of the mental training aiming at deliverance. Hence we may summarise this part of the discourse by saying that *our social conduct strongly affects the chances of our spiritual progress.*

The nature of that influence is illustrated by the simile of the cloth. If the texture of our mind is tarnished by blemishes in our social behaviour, "the new colouring" of *higher mentality (adhicitta)* and *higher wisdom (adhipaññā)* cannot penetrate. The stains that soil the single strands of thought will show through the superficial colouring; and besides, the impure matter will reduce the porosity of the tissue, i. e. the receptivity of our mind, and thus prevent full absorption of any results gained in meditation or understanding. Through the accumulating "waste products" of uninhibited defilements, a mental atmosphere is created that resists any depth penetration of spiritual forces and values.

First, in accordance with the method of Satipaṭṭhāna, right mindfulness, the presence of the defilements in one's behaviour has to be clearly noticed and honestly acknowledged, without attempts at evasion, at minimizing or self-justification, for instance, by giving them more "respectable" names. This is what is implied in the words of the discourse: "*Knowing* (the respective blemish) to be a defilement of the mind . . ." Such knowledge by itself may often discourage the recurrence of the defilements or weaken the strength of their manifestations. According to the Buddhist Teachers of Old (see Note 4, para. 1), this knowledge should be extended to the nature of the defilements, the causes and circumstances of their arising, their cessation, and the means of effecting their cessation. This is an example of how to apply to an actual situation the formula of the Four Noble Truths as embodied in the contemplation of mind-objects *(dhammānupassanā)* of the Satipaṭṭhāna Sutta. Another example is the application of the four truths to higher states of mind, the Divine Abidings, for the purpose of developing insight (Sec. 13 and notes 13, 14).

When the Noble Disciple, on attaining to one of the higher paths, sees himself freed from the defilements, deep joy will arise in him, enthusiasm for the goal and the way, and an unshakable confidence in the Triple Gem. So says our text (Sec. 6-10). But a foretaste of all these fruits and blessings can already be gained by him who has succeeded in noticeably weakening and reducing the defilements. Such enthusiasm and strengthened confidence, being derived from his personal experience, will be of great value to him, adding wings to his further progress. To the extent of his experience, he will have verified for himself the virtues of the Dhamma:

"Well proclaimed by the Blessed One is the Dhamma, realisable here and now, possessed of immediate result, bidding you come and see, accessible, and knowable individually by the wise."

* * *

For rendering this discourse, use has been made chiefly of the translation by the Venerable Ñāṇamoli Thera (from an unpublished manuscript), and also of the translations by the Venerable Soma Thera and I. B. Horner. Grateful acknowledgement is offered to these able translators. For some key passages, however, the Editor decided to use his own version, partly for the reason of conformity with the commentarial explanations. The Notes have been supplied by the Editor. In these Notes, it was thought desirable to furnish the commentarial references supporting the renderings chosen, and in these cases the inclusion of Pali words was unavoidable. But an effort has been made to make these notes intelligible and helpful to readers who are not familiar with the Pali language as well.

The Simile of the Cloth
(Vatthūpama Sutta)

1. Thus have I heard. Once the Blessed One was staying at Sāvatthi, in Jeta's Grove, Anāthapindika's monastery. There he addressed the monks thus: "Monks." —"Venerable sir," they replied. The Blessed One said this:

2. "Monks, suppose a cloth were stained and dirty, and a dyer dipped it in some dye or other, whether blue or yellow or red or pink, it would take the dye badly and be impure in colour. And why is that? Because the cloth was not clean. So too, monks, when the mind is defiled,[1] an unhappy destination (in a future existence) may be expected.

"Monks, suppose a cloth were clean and bright, and a dyer dipped it in some dye or other, whether blue or yellow or red or pink, it would take the dye well and be pure in colour. And why is that? Because the cloth was clean. So too, monks, when the mind is undefiled, a happy destination (in a future existence) may be expected.

3. "And what, monks, are the defilements of the mind?[2] (1) Covetousness and unrighteous greed are a defilement of the mind; (2) ill will is a defilement of the mind; (3) anger is a defilement of the mind; (4) hostility . . . (5) denigration . . . (6) domineering . . . (7) envy . . . (8) jealousy . . . (9) hypocrisy . . . (10) fraud . . . (11) obstinacy . . . (12) presumption . . . (13) conceit

... (14) arrogance ... (15) vanity ... (16) negligence is a defilement of the mind.[3]

4. "Knowing, monks, covetousness and unrighteous greed to be a defilement of the mind, the monk abandons them.[4] Knowing ill will to be a defilement of the mind, he abandons it. Knowing anger to be a defilement of the mind, he abandons it. Knowing hostility to be a defilement of the mind, he abandons it. Knowing denigration to be a defilement of the mind, he abandons it. Knowing domineering to be a defilement of the mind, he abandons it. Knowing envy to be a defilement of the mind, he abandons it. Knowing jealousy to be a defilement of the mind, he abandons it. Knowing hypocrisy to be a defilement of the mind, he abandons it. Knowing fraud to be a defilement of the mind, he abandons it. Knowing obstinacy to be a defilement of the mind, he abandons it. Knowing presumption to be a defilement of the mind, he abandons it. Knowing conceit to be a defilement of the mind, he abandons it. Knowing arrogance to be a defilement of the mind, he abandons it. Knowing vanity to be a defilement of the mind, he abandons it. Knowing negligence to be a defilement of the mind, he abandons it.

5. "When in the monk who thus knows that covetousness and unrighteous greed are a defilement of the mind, this covetousness and unrighteous greed have been abandoned; when in him who thus knows that ill will is a defilement of the mind, this ill will has been abandoned; ... when in him who thus knows that negligence is a defilement of the mind, this negligence has been abandoned—[5]

6. —he thereupon gains unwavering confidence in the Buddha[6] thus: 'Thus indeed is the Blessed One: he is accomplished, fully enlightened, endowed with (clear) vision and (virtuous) conduct, sublime, knower of the worlds, the incomparable guide of men who are tractable, the teacher of gods and men, enlightened and blessed.'

7. —he gains unwavering confidence in the Dhamma thus: 'Well proclaimed by the Blessed One is the Dhamma, realisable here and now, possessed of immediate result, bidding you come and see, accessible and knowable individually by the wise.

8. —he gains unwavering confidence in the Sangha thus: 'The Sangha of the Blessed One's disciples has entered on the good way, has entered on the straight way, has entered on the true way, has entered on the proper way; that is to say, the four pairs of men, the eight types of persons; this Sangha of the Blessed One's disciples is worthy of gifts, worthy of hospitality, worthy of offerings, worthy of reverential salutation, the incomparable field of merit for the world.'

9. "When he has given up, renounced, let go, abandoned and relinquished (the defilements) in part,[7] he knows: 'I am endowed with unwavering confidence in the Buddha . . . in the Dhamma . . . in the Sangha; and he gains enthusiasm for the goal, gains enthusiasm for the Dhamma,[8] gains gladness connected with the Dhamma. When he is gladdened, joy is born in him; being joyous in mind, his body becomes tranquil; his body being tranquil, he feels

happiness; and the mind of him who is happy becomes concentrated.⁹

10. "He knows: 'I have given up, renounced, let go, abandoned and relinquished (the defilements) in part'; and he gains enthusiasm for the goal, gains enthusiasm for the Dhamma, gains gladness connected with the Dhamma. When he is gladdened, joy is born in him; being joyous in mind, his body becomes tranquil; when his body is tranquil, he feels happiness; and the mind of him who is happy becomes concentrated.

11. "If, monks, a monk of such virtue, such concentration and such wisdom¹⁰ eats almsfood consisting of choice hill-rice together with various sauces and curries, even that will be no obstacle for him.¹¹

"Just as cloth that is stained and dirty becomes clean and bright with the help of pure water, or just as gold becomes clean and bright with the help of a furnace, so too, if a monk of such virtue, such concentration and such wisdom eats almsfood consisting of choice hill-rice together with various sauces and curries, even that will be no obstacle for him.

12. "He abides, having suffused with a mind of loving-kindness¹² one direction of the world, likewise the second, likewise the third, likewise the fourth, and so above, below, around and everywhere, and to all as to himself; he abides suffusing the entire universe with loving-kindness, with a mind grown great, lofty, boundless and free from enmity and ill will.

"He abides, having suffused with a mind of compassion . . . of sympathetic joy . . . of equanimity one direction of the world, likewise the second, likewise the third, likewise the fourth, and so above, below, around and everywhere, and to all as to himself; he abides suffusing the entire universe with equanimity, with a mind grown great, lofty, boundless and free from enmity and ill will.

13. "He understands what exists, what is low, what is excellent,[13] and what escape there is from this (whole) field of perception.[14]

14. "When he knows and sees[15] in this way, his mind becomes liberated from the canker of sensual desire, liberated from the canker of becoming, liberated from the canker of ignorance.[16] When liberated, there is knowledge: 'It is liberated'; and he knows: 'Birth is exhausted, the life of purity has been lived, the task is done, there is no more of this to come.' Such a monk is called 'one bathed with the inner bathing.'"[17]

15. Now at that time the brahmin Sundarika Bhāradvāja[18] was seated not far from the Blessed One, and he spoke to the Blessed One thus: "But does Master Gotama go to the Bahukā River to bathe?"

"What good, brahmin, is the Bahukā River? What can the Bahukā River do?"

"Truly, Master Gotama, many people believe that the Bahukā River gives purification, many people believe that the Bahukā River gives merit. For in the Bahukā River many people wash away the evil deeds they have done."

16. Then the Blessed One addressed the brahmin Sundarika Bharadvāja in these stanzas:[19]

"Bahukā and Adhikakkā,[20]
Gayā and Sundarikā,
Payāga and Sarassati,
And the stream Bahumati—
A fool may there forever bathe,
Yet will not purify his black deeds.

What can Sundarikā bring to pass?
What can the Payāga and the Bahukā?
They cannot purify an evil-doer,
A man performing brutal and cruel acts.

One pure in heart has evermore
The Feast of Cleansing[21] and the Holy Day;[22]
One pure in heart who does good deeds
Has his observances perfect for all times.

It is here, O brahmin, that you should bathe[23]
To make yourself a safe refuge for all beings.
And if you speak no untruth,
Nor work any harm for breathing things,

Nor take what is not offered,
With faith and with no avarice,
To Gayā gone, what would it do for you?
Let any well your Gayā be!"

17. When this was said, the brahmin Sundarika Bhāradvāja spoke thus:

"Magnificent, Master Gotama, magnificent, Master Gotama! The Dhamma has been made clear in many ways by Master Gotama, as though he were righting the overthrown, revealing the hidden, showing the way to one who is lost, or holding up a lamp in the dark for those with eyesight to see forms.

18. "I go to Master Gotama for refuge, and to the Dhamma, and to the Sangha. May I receive the (first ordination of) going forth under Master Gotama, may I receive the full admission!

19. And the brahmin Sundarika Bhāradvāja received the (first ordination of) going forth under the Blessed One, and he received the full admission. And not long after his full admission, dwelling alone, secluded, diligent, ardent and resolute, the venerable Bhāradvāja by his own realisation understood and attained in this very life that supreme goal of the pure life, for which men of good family go forth from home life into homelessness. And he had direct knowledge thus: "Birth is exhausted, the pure life has been lived, the task is done, there is no more of this to come."

And the venerable Bhāradvāja became one of the Arahats.

Notes

1. *"So too, monks, if the mind is defiled . . ."*
Comy: "It may be asked why the Buddha had given this simile of the soiled cloth. He did so to show that effort brings great results. A cloth soiled by dirt that is adventitious (i. e. comes from outside; *āgantukehi malehi*), if it is washed can again become clean because of the cloth's natural purity. But in the case of what is naturally black, as for instance (black) goat's fur, any effort (of washing it) will be in vain. Similarly, the mind too is soiled by adventitious defilements (*āgantukehi kilesehi*). But originally, at the phases of rebirth(-consciousness) and the (sub-conscious) life-continuum, it is pure throughout (*pakatiyā pana sakale pi paṭisandhi-bhavaṅga-vāre paṇḍaram eva*). As it was said (by the Enlightened One): 'This mind, monks, is luminous, but it becomes soiled by adventitious defilements' (Anguttara Nikāya I). But by cleansing it one can make it more luminous, and effort therein is not in vain."

2. *"Defilements of the mind"* (*cittassa upakkilesā*). Comy.: "When explaining the mental defilements, why did the Blessed One mention greed first? Because it arises first. For with all beings wherever they arise, up to the level of the (Brahma heaven of the) Pure Abodes, it is first greed that arises by way of lust for existence (*bhava-nikanti*). Then the other defilements will appear, being produced according to circumstances. The defilements of mind, however, are not limited to the sixteen mentioned in

this discourse. But one should understand that, by indicating here the method, all defilements are included." Sub.Comy. mentions the following additional defilements: fear, cowardice, shamelessness and lack of scruples, insatiability, evil ambitions, etc.

3. The Sixteen Defilements of Mind

1. *abhijjhā-visama-lobha*, covetousness and unrighteous greed
2. *byāpāda*, ill will
3. *kodha*, anger
4. *upanāha*, hostility or malice
5. *makkha*, denigration or detraction; contempt
6. *paḷāsa*, domineering or presumption
7. *issā*, envy
8. *macchariya*, jealousy, or avarice; selfishness
9. *māyā*, hypocrisy or deceit
10. *sāṭheyya*, fraud
11. *thambha*, obstinacy, obduracy
12. *sārambha*, presumption or rivalry; impetuosity
13. *māna*, conceit
14. *atimāna*, arrogance, haughtiness
15. *mada*, vanity or pride
16. *pamāda*, negligence or heedlessness; in social behaviour, this leads to lack of consideration.

The defilements (3) to (16) appear frequently as a group in the discourses, e. g. in Majjh. 3; while in Majjh. 8 (reproduced in this publication) No. 15 is omitted. A list of seventeen defilements appears regularly in each last discourse of Books 3 to 11 of the Anguttara Nikāya, which carry the title *Rāgapeyyāla*, the Repetitive Text on Greed (etc.). In these texts of the Anguttara Nikāya, the first two defilements in the above list are called greed *(lobha)* and hate *(dosa)*, to which delusion *(moha)* is added; all the fourteen other defilements are identical with the above list.

4. *"Knowing covetousness and unrighteous greed to be a defilement of the mind, the monk abandons them."*

Knowing (viditvā). Sub.Comy.: "Having known it either through the incipient wisdom *(pubbabhāgapaññā* of the worldling, i. e. before attaining to Stream-entry) or through the wisdom of the two lower paths (Stream-entry and Once-returning). He knows the defilements as to their nature, cause, cessation and means of effecting cessation." This application of the formula of the Four Noble Truths to the defilements deserves close attention.

Abandons them (pajahati). Comy.: "He abandons the respective defilement through (his attainment of) the noble path where there is 'abandoning by eradication' *(samucchedappahāna-vasena ariya-maggena)*," which according to Sub.Comy. is the "final abandoning" *(accantappahāna)*. Before the attainment of the noble paths, all "abandoning" of defilements is of a temporary nature. See Nyanatiloka Thera, *Buddhist Dictionary*, s. v. *pahāna*.

According to the Comy., the sixteen defilements are finally abandoned by the noble paths (or stages of sanctity) in the following order:

"By the *path of Stream-entry (sotāpatti-magga)* are abandoned: (5) denigration, (6) domineering, (7) envy, (8) jealousy, (9) hypocrisy, (10) fraud.

"By the *path of Non-returning (anāgāmi-magga)*: (2) ill will, (3) anger, (4) malice, (16) negligence.

"By the *path of Arahatship (arahatta-magga)*: (1) covetousness and unrighteous greed, (11) obstinacy, (12) presumption, (13) conceit, (14) arrogance, (15) vanity."

If, in the last group of terms, covetousness is taken in a restricted sense as referring only to the craving for the five sense objects, it is finally abandoned by the path of Non-returning; and this is according to Comy. the meaning intended here. All greed, however, including the hankering after fine-material and immaterial existence, is eradicated only on the path of Arahatship; hence the classification under the latter in the list above.

Comy. repeatedly stresses that wherever in our text "abandoning" is mentioned, reference is to the Non-returner *(anāgāmi)*; for also in the case of defilements overcome on Stream-entry (see above), the states of mind which produce those defilements are eliminated only by the path of Non-returning.

5. Comy. emphasises the connection of this paragraph with the following, saying that the statements on each of the sixteen defilements should be connected with the next paragraphs, e. g. "when in him . . . ill will has been abandoned, he thereupon gains unwavering confidence . . ." Hence the grammatical construction of the original Pali passage—though rather awkward in English—has been retained in this translation.

The disciple's direct experience of being freed of this or that defilement becomes for him a living test of his former still imperfectly proven trust in the Buddha, Dhamma and Sangha. Now this trust has become a firm conviction, an unshakable confidence, based on experience.

6. *"Unwavering confidence"* (*aveccappasāda*). Comy.: "unshakable and immutable trust." Confidence of that nature is not attained before Stream-entry because only at that stage is the fetter of sceptical doubt (*vicikicchā-saṁyojana*) finally eliminated. Unwavering confidence in the Buddha, Dhamma and Sangha are three of four characteristic qualities of a Stream-winner (*sotāpannassa angāni*); the fourth is unbroken morality, which may be taken to be implied in Sec. 9 of our discourse referring to the relinquishment of the defilements.

7. *"When he has given up . . . (the defilements) in part"* (*yatodhi*): that is, to the extent to which the respective defilements are eliminated by the paths of sanctitude (see Note 4). *Odhi*: limit, limitation. *yatodhi* = *yato odhi*; another reading: *yathodhi* = *yathā-odhi*.

Bhikkhu Ñāṇamoli translates this paragraph thus: "And whatever (from among those imperfections) has, according to the limitation (set by whichever of the first three paths he has attained), been given up, has been (forever) dropped, let go, abandoned, relinquished."

In the *Vibhanga* of the Abhidhamma Pitaka, we read in the chapter *Jhāna-vibhanga*: "He is a bhikkhu because he has abandoned defilements limitedly; or because he has abandoned defilements without limitation" *(odhiso kilesānaṁ pahānā bhikkhu; anodhiso kilesānaṁ pahānā bhikkhu).*

8. *"Gains enthusiasm for the goal, gains enthusiasm for the Dhamma" (labhati atthavedaṁ labhati dhammavedaṁ).*

Comy.: "When reviewing *(paccavekkhato)** the abandonment of the defilements and his unwavering confidence, strong joy arises in the Non-returner in the thought: 'Such and such defilements are now abandoned by me.' It is like the joy of a king who learns that a rebellion in the frontier region has been quelled."

---

*"Reviewing" *(paccavekkhanā)* is a commentarial term, but is derived, apart from actual meditative experience, from close scrutiny of sutta passages like our present one. "Reviewing" may occur immediately after attainment of the jhānas or the paths and fruitions (e. g. the last sentence of Sec. 14), or as a reviewing of the defilements abandoned (as in Sec. 10) or those remaining. See *Visuddhimagga,* transl. by Ñāṇamoli, p. 789.

Enthusiasm (veda). According to Comy., the word *veda* occurs in the Pali texts with three connotations: 1. (Vedic) scripture *(gantha)*, 2. joy *(somanassa)*, 3. knowledge *(ñāṇa)*. "Here it signifies joy and the knowledge connected with that joy."

Attha (rendered here as "goal") and *dhamma* are a frequently occurring pair of terms obviously intended to supplement each other. Often they mean letter *(dhamma)* and spirit (or meaning: *attha)* of the doctrine; but this hardly fits here. These two terms occur also among the four kinds of analytic knowledge *(paṭisambhidā-ñāṇa;* or knowledge of doctrinal discrimination). *Attha-paṭisambhidā* is explained as the discriminative knowledge of "the result of a cause"; while *dhamma-paṭisambhidā* is concerned with the cause or condition.

The Comy. applies now the same interpretation to our present textual passage, saying: "*Attha-veda* is the enthusiasm arisen in him who reviews his unwavering confidence; *dhamma-veda* is the enthusiasm arisen in him who reviews 'the abandonment of the defilement in part,' which is the cause of that unwavering confidence . . ." Hence the two terms refer to "the joy that has as its object the unwavering confidence in the Buddha, and so forth; and the joy inherent in the knowledge (of the abandonment; *somanassa-maya ñāṇa*)."

Our rendering of *attha* (Skt.:*artha*) by "goal" is supported by Comy.: "The unwavering confidence is called *attha* because it has to be reached *(araṇiyato)*, i. e. to be approached *(upagantabbato),*" in the sense of a limited goal, or resultant blessing.

Cf. Ang. 5:10: *tasmiṁ dhamme attha-paṭisaṁvedī ca hoti dhammapaṭisaṁvedī ca; tassa atthapaṭisaṁvedino dhammapaṭisaṁvedino pāmojjaṁ jāyati* . . . This text continues, as our present discourse does, with the arising of joy (or rapture; *pīti*) from gladness (*pāmojja*). *Attha* and *dhamma* refer here to the meaning and text of the Buddha word.

9. The Pali equivalents for this series of terms* are: 1. *pāmojja* (gladness), 2. *pīti* (joy or rapture), 3. *passaddhi* (tranquillity), 4. *sukha* (happiness), 5. *samādhi* (concentration). Nos. 2, 3, 5 are factors of enlightenment (*bojjhanga*). The function of tranquillity is here the calming of any slight bodily and mental unrest resulting from rapturous joy, and so transforming the latter into serene happiness followed by meditative absorption. This frequently occurring passage illustrates the importance given in the Buddha's Teaching to happiness as a necessary condition for the attainment of concentration and of spiritual progress in general.

10. "*Of such virtue, such concentration, such wisdom*" (*evaṁ-sīlo evaṁ-dhammo evaṁ-pañño*). Comy.: "This refers to the (three) parts (of the Noble Eightfold Path), namely, virtue, concentration and wisdom (*sīla-, samādhi-, paññā-kkhandha*), associated (here) with the path of Non-returning." Comy. merely refers *dhammo* to the path-category of concentration (*samādhi-kkhandha*). Sub.Comy. quotes a parallel

---

* Here the noun forms are given, while the original has, in some cases, the verbal forms.

passage "*evaṁ-dhammā ti Bhagavanto ahesuṁ,*" found in the Mahāpadāna Sutta (Dīgha 15), the Acchariya-abbhūtadhamma Sutta (Majjh. 123), and the Nālanda Sutta of the Satipaṭṭhāna Saṁyutta. The Dīgha Comy. explains *samādhi-pakkha-dhammā* as "mental states belonging to concentration."

11. *"No obstacle,"* i. e. for the attainment of the path and fruition (of Arahatship), says Comy. For a Non-returner who has eliminated the fetter of sense-desire, there is no attachment to tasty food.

12. *"With a mind of loving-kindness"* (*mettā-sahagatena cetasā*). This, and the following, refer to the four Divine Abidings (*brahma-vihāra*). On these see Wheel Nos. 6 and 7.

13. *"He understands what exists, what is low, what is excellent"* (*so 'atthi idaṁ atthi hīnaṁ atthi paṇītaṁ . . .' pajānāti*).

Comy.: "Having shown the Non-returner's meditation on the Divine Abidings, the Blessed One now shows his practice of insight (*vipassanā*), aiming at Arahatship; and he indicates his attainment of it by the words: 'He understands what exists,' etc. This Non-returner, having arisen from the meditation on any of the four Divine Abidings, defines as 'mind' (*nāma*) those very states of the Divine Abidings and the mental factors associated with them. He then defines as 'matter' (*rūpa*) the heart base (*hadaya-vatthu*) being the physical support (of mind) and the four elements which, on their part, are the support of the heart base. In that way he defines as 'matter' the elements and corporeal phenomena derived from them *(bhūtupādāyadhammā)*. When defining 'mind and matter' in this manner, *'he understands what exists'* (atthi idan'ti; lit. 'There is this'). Hereby a definition of the truth of suffering has been given."

"Then, in comprehending the origin of that suffering, he understands *'what is low.'* Thereby the truth of the origin of suffering has been defined. Further, by investigating the means of giving it up, he understands *'what is excellent.'* Hereby the truth of the path has been defined."

14. ". . . *and what escape there is from this (whole) field of perception*" *(atthi uttari imassa saññāgatassa nissaraṇaṁ)*. Comy.: "He knows: 'There is Nibbāna as an escape beyond that perception of the Divine Abidings attained by me.' Hereby the truth of cessation has been defined."

15. Comy.: "When, by insight-wisdom *(vipassanā-paññā)*, he thus *knows* the Four Noble Truths in these four ways (i. e. 'what exists,' etc.); and when he thus *sees* them by path-wisdom *(magga-paññā)*."

16. *Kāmāsava bhavāsava avijjāsava*. The mention of liberation from the cankers *(āsava)* indicates the monk's attainment of Arahatship which is also called "exhaustion of the cankers" *(āsavakkhaya)*.

17. *"Bathed with the inner bathing"* (sināto antarena sinānena). According to the Comy., the Buddha used

this phrase to rouse the attention of the brahmin Sundarika Bhāradvāja, who was in the assembly and who believed in purification by ritual bathing. The Buddha foresaw that if he were to speak in praise of "purification by bathing," the brahmin would feel inspired to take ordination under him and finally attain to Arahatship.

18. *Bhāradvāja* was the clan name of the brahmin. *Sundarika* was the name of the river to which that brahmin ascribed purifying power. See also the Sundarika-Bhāradvāja Sutta in the *Sutta Nipāta*.

19. Based on Bhikkhu Ñāṇamoli's version, with a few alterations.

20. Three are fords; the other four are rivers.

21. The text has *Phaggu* which is a day of brahminic purification in the month of Phagguna (February-March). Ñāṇamoli translates it as "Feast of Spring."

22. *Uposatha*.

23. *"It is here, O brahmin, that you should bathe."* Comy.: i. e. in the Buddha's Dispensation, in the waters of the Noble Eightfold Path.

In the *Psalms of the Sisters (Therīgāthā)*, the nun Puṇṇikā speaks to a brahmin as follows:

"Nay now, who, ignorant to the ignorant,
Hath told thee this: that water-baptism
From evil kamma can avail to free?

Why then the fishes and the tortoises,
The frogs, the watersnake, the crocodiles
And all that haunt the water straight to heaven
Will go. Yea, all who evil kamma work—
Butchers of sheep and swine, fishers, hunters of game,
Thieves, murderers—so they but splash themselves
With water, are from evil kamma free!"

Transl. by C. A. F. Rhys Davids
From *Early Buddhist Poetry*, ed. I. B. Horner
Publ. by Ananda Semage, Colombo 11

THE DISCOURSE ON EFFACEMENT

Introduction

The Buddha's Discourse on Effacement (Sallekha Sutta; quoted as M. 8) is the eighth of the Collection of Middle Length Texts (Majjhima Nikāya). Its subject matter is closely connected with that of the preceding text, The Simile of the Cloth (M. 7), and these two discourses supplement each other in several ways.

The Simile of the Cloth speaks of sixteen defilements of social conduct as impeding the progress on the higher stages of the path to deliverance. The present Discourse on Effacement widens the range to forty-four detrimental qualities of mind which must be effaced. These include thirteen of the sixteen defilements in M. 7,* but they go beyond the realm of social ethics, extending also to the hindrances, the path factors, etc.; and special attention is given to the effacement of wrong views (Sec. 12, No. 44). This discourse supplements M. 7 also by dealing with the *practical methods* of effacement, from the very beginning with thought-arising (Sec. 13), on to avoidance (Sec. 14), etc.; and these methods apply as well to the purification from the sixteen defilements given in M. 7. On the other hand, the 7th discourse gives more details about the higher stages of progress that follow after the initial and partial purification.

---

* Items 1-11 and 16 of list in Sec. 3 of M. 7.

(Sec. 12) "Effacement" means the radical removal of detrimental qualities of mind. The forty-four Modes of Effacement (as we may call them) are enumerated in this discourse no less than five times, and the first formulation (in Sec. 12) is very significant: "Others will be harmful, we shall not be harmful here," and so forth through all the other items. This bespeaks of the Buddha's realistic outlook as befitting a world that cannot be improved by mere wishing nor by "preaching at it." There is no use nor hope in waiting for our neighbour to change his ways. "Cleanup campaigns" should start at our own door, and then the neighbours may well be more responsive to our own example than to our preaching. Besides, if the aim is the radical effacement of mental defilements, we cannot afford to waste time and be deviated from our task by side-long glances at the behaviour of others. Here lurks, in addition, the danger of pride. Hence the *Sutta Nipāta* (v. 918) warns that "though possessing many a virtue one should not compare oneself with others by deeming oneself better or equal or inferior." It is a "virtue that squints" (Chungtze) that will deprive the progress on the path of the element of self-forgetting joyous spontaneity.

There is yet another reason for the injunction not to look to others' behaviour or misbehaviour, and this applies particularly to the defilements of social conduct mentioned in the Simile of the Cloth. It is quite human to feel disappointed if one's selflessness, kindliness, modesty, and so on, do not find much response in the behaviour of others. Such disappointment may well discourage a person not only from continuing to live according to his moral standard, but also from advancing further on the road to selflessness towards higher states of mental development. Such a person, after an initial disappointment, may easily be led to retire into the role of the "disgruntled moralist," as a respectable cloak for an egocentric life. Here we meet the limitations and risks of a morality solely motivated by the social response to it. To avoid such a blind alley on one's road of progress, it is important to make from the very beginning that "declaration of moral independence," which we may summarize thus: "Others may act, speak and think wrongly, but we shall act, speak and think rightly—thus effacement can be done."

(Sec. 13) But the Buddha, as a knower of the human heart, was well aware that such a single or even repeated resolve will not always be strong enough to stir people into action. Hence, as an encouragement to those who may feel disheartened by their failures, he speaks now of the importance of the "arising of thoughts" aiming at carrying out those acts of effacement. But again, these thoughts will not be effective unless they are regularly and systematically cultivated and are not allowed to lapse into oblivion. Then gradually they will be absorbed by our mind and heart, and we shall fully identify ourselves with those values. In that way these thoughts and aspirations will grow stronger and will be able to overcome the resistance of inertia and antagonistic forces, from within and without. The Master said: "To whatsoever one frequently gives attention and repeatedly reflects on, to that the mind will turn" (M. 19). The great German mystic of the Middle Ages, Meister Eckhart, goes even a step further by saying: "If you do not have the longing, have at least a longing for the longing."

(Sec. 14) Next to cultivating "the heart's resolve," the first direct step towards effacing the defilements is to know them, that is, the clear and honest confrontation with them in one's own mind, as we pointed out when considering the Simile of the Cloth (see the Introduction to it, p. 3). This will surely help in preventing their re-arising. But for strengthening and extending that effect, it is necessary to cultivate also the positive counterparts of those forty-four negative qualities, as taught in the instruction on avoidance. The Buddha's formulation in this section conveys the encouraging word that there actually exists such a road for avoiding or circumventing the wrong path. The Buddha said: "If it were not possible to give up what is evil, I would not tell you to give it up; if it were not possible to develop what is good, I would not tell you to develop it" (Ang. 2:2).

In the field of insight *(vipassanā)*, this method is called "abandoning by the opposite" *(tadangapahāna)*, but by extension we may apply this term also to the wider range of our present context.

(Sec. 15) Apart from its highest purpose, the cultivation of positive qualities of mind is, on any level, a road of progress, a "way that leads upwards." It brings results here and now, and leads to a favourable and happy rebirth. It will preserve and unfold what is best in us and prevent it from deterioration. Considering the fearful possibilities in man's own nature and in the realms of existence, this is no mean benefit of training the mind for the final effacement of defilements, even if the results remain modest for a long time.

(Sec. 16) For him who has advanced so far, there is now the warning in the text that he should not set himself up as a saviour of others while "there is still more to do" for him. At this stage, the disciple may have effected some partial effacement, but still the fires of greed, hatred and delusion are not quenched in him; or, to express it with the other metaphor here used, he is still immersed in the mire. Though his chances for freeing himself from that bog of saṁsāra have improved, any wrong step, or just his negligence and lack of persevering effort, may cause a setback. Hence a determined effort should now be made for the final "quenching," for radical effacement.

(Secs. 1-11) This warning against an overestimation of one's position links up with the first sections of our text which we have still to consider. They likewise deal with the overrating of one's achievements, here in the fields of insight and meditative absorptions. Even initial steps in these fields may result in experiences having such a strong impact on the mind that it is psychologically understandable if they lead to overestimation. This does not necessarily mean overrating oneself through pride, but overrating the position of one's achievements on the path of progress. One may believe them to be complete in their field while they are only partial; or to be final while they are only temporary suppressions.

(Sec. 3) If confronted with "wrong views on self and world," one will, at first sight, be inclined to believe that any trace of them in oneself can be eliminated by intellectual refutation, that is, by proving to one's own satisfaction that they are untenable. And if one has a firm conviction in the truth of the Dhamma, it will be easy to assume that one has discarded wrong views for good. In that overestimation one may even go as far as to believe that one has entirely overcome the first of the ten fetters, personality-belief, and hence is on the way to Stream-entry, or has even reached it. But this can never be achieved on the intellectual level alone, nor even on the first stages of insight-meditation, which in themselves are no mean achievement.

Misconceptions of self and world, which may be quite instinctive and unphilosophical, are deeply anchored in man's nature. They are rooted not only in his intellectual opinions (*diṭṭhi*), but also in his cravings (*taṇhā*) and in his pride and self-assertion (*māna*). All these three roots of wrong attitudes identify the alleged self or ego with the five aggregates (*khandha*) comprising personality-and-environment. These wrong attitudes towards self and world may manifest themselves on various levels: as casual thought-arisings, as a habitual bias, and in words and deeds (see Note 8). Only if the self-identification with the actual "objects of wrong views," i. e. the five aggregates, is radically dissolved on the stage of Stream-entry, can it be said that wrong views of self and world have been totally eliminated, together with the bias towards them. As also craving and pride are involved in the formation of wrong views, efforts for their effacement have to be undertaken also on the level of ethical behaviour. Hence the ethical part of the forty-four Modes of Effacement has validity also for the removal of wrong views.

(Secs. 4-11) The eight meditative attainments lift the human consciousness to sublime heights of refinement; yet, in the case of each, the Buddha emphatically says that they are not states of effacement, as he understands them. They can effect only temporary subsidence of defilements, and if unsupported by mature virtue and insight, they cannot penetrate deep enough into the recesses of the mind for a radical removal of moral and intellectual defilements. It comes as a kind of anti-climax that after mentioning those sublime meditative attainments, the Buddha now speaks (in Sec. 12) of such quite "ordinary and earth-bound" ethical qualities as harmlessness, and ascribes to them, and not to the meditative absorptions, the capacity of leading to effacement. This juxtaposition implies, indeed, a very strong emphasis on the necessity of a sound ethical foundation for any spiritual progress. Often we find that mystic thought, in India and elsewhere, evolving a monistic system from wrongly interpreted unificatory meditative experience, has either ignored ethics or found it difficult to give it a convincing place and motivation in its system. The exultation of mystic experience also often leads the meditator to a premature feeling of having gone "beyond good and evil." Such developments illustrate the wisdom of the Buddha in insisting on a sound ethical basis instead of an exclusive reliance on mystic experience.

* * *

When examining closely the structure of this discourse, we find in it a repeated balancing of contrasting attitudes of mind and of complementary qualities required for progress on the path. Just now we have observed that meditative achievements have to be balanced with deeply rooted ethical virtues, which will also provide a link between the "lone meditator" and "common humanity." With the last of the forty-four Modes of Effacement the effacing of wrong views is taken up again, linking up with the beginning of the discourse and balancing the stress on ethical values in most of the other modes. In the phrasing of that last mode we note the stress laid on the overcoming of opinionatedness and tenacity. This points to the fact that, for the initial "loosening up" and final overcoming of wrong views, the following ethical modes are of decisive importance: amenability (34) and an increasing freedom from a domineering attitude (27), obstinacy (32) and arrogance (33).

The entire discourse seems to be designed to meet, in a very thorough manner, two opposite psychological obstacles on the path: discouragement in the face of its difficulties, and overrating of partial results. The first part of the discourse (Secs. 1-11) deals with the latter extreme, by stressing the limitations of initial and partial progress. But for meeting any discouragement caused by these warnings, the Compassionate Master speaks of the value of seemingly simple ethical virtues and stresses the importance of the heart's earnest resolve (Sec. 13) as the first step which anyone can take who is serious about treading the path of actual effacement.

These features of the discourse, without being stated explicitly, are inherent in its very structure. They will reveal themselves by a close scrutiny as here attempted, and particularly by the actual practice of the teachings concerned. The Buddha appears here as the great Teacher of the Middle Path and the incomparable guide of men's hearts, deeply concerned that those who tread the path may avoid the pitfalls of extreme emotional reactions and of one-sided emphasis on any single aspect of the threefold totality of training: in virtue, concentration and insight.

* * *

As in the preceding discourse, the rendering of the present one also has been chiefly based on Ñāṇamoli Thera's manuscript translation. To a lesser extent use has been made of phrasings by Soma Thera and I. B. Horner; and for some passages the Editor's own version has been included.

The Discourse on Effacement
(Sallekha Sutta)

1. Thus have I heard. Once the Blessed One was staying at Sāvatthi, in Jeta's Grove, Anāthapindika's monastery.

2. Then one evening the venerable Mahā-Cunda[1] rose from meditative seclusion and went to the Blessed One. Having paid homage to him, he sat down at one side and spoke thus to the Blessed One:

3. "Venerable sir, there are these various views that arise in the world concerning self-doctrines or world-doctrines.[2] Does the abandoning and discarding of such views come about in a monk who is only at the beginning of his (meditative) reflections?"[3]

"Cunda, as to those several views that arise in the world concerning self-doctrines and world-doctrines, if (the object) in which[4] these views arise, in which they underlie and become active,[5] is seen with right wisdom[6] as it actually is,[7] thus: 'This is not mine,[8] this I am not,[9] this is not my self'[10]—then the abandoning of these views, their discarding,[11] takes place in him (who thus sees).

The Eight Attainments

4. "It may be, Cunda, that some monk, detached from sense-objects, detached from unsalutary ideas, enters into the first absorption that is born of detachment, accompanied by thought-conception and discursive thinking, and filled with rapture and

joy, and he then might think: 'I am abiding in effacement.' But in the Noble One's discipline it is not these (attainments) that are called 'effacement'; in the Noble One's discipline they are called 'abidings in ease here and now.'[1][2]

5. "It may be that after the stilling of thought-conception and discursive thinking, he gains the inner tranquillity and harmony of the second absorption that is free of thought-conception and discursive thinking, born of concentration and filled with rapture and joy; and he then might think: 'I am abiding in effacement.' But in the Noble One's discipline it is not these (attainments) that are called 'effacement'; in the Noble One's discipline they are called 'abidings in ease here and now.'

6. "It may be that after the fading away of rapture, the monk dwells in equanimity, mindful and clearly aware, and he experiences a happiness in his body of which the Noble Ones say: 'Happily lives he who dwells in equanimity and is mindful!'—that third absorption he wins; and he then might think: 'I am abiding in effacement.' But in the Noble One's discipline it is not these (attainments)) that are called 'effacement'; in the Noble One's discipline they are called 'abidings in ease here and now.'

7. "It may be that with the abandoning of pleasure and pain, and with the previous disappearance of joy and grief, he enters upon and abides in the fourth absorption, which is beyond pleasure and pain and has purity of mindfulness due to equanimity; and he then might think: 'I am abiding in effacement.' But in

the Noble One's discipline it is not these (attainments) that are called 'effacement'; in the Noble One's discipline they are called 'abidings in ease here and now.'

8. "It may be that, with the entire transcending of perceptions of corporealty,[13] with the disappearance of perceptions of sense-response,[14] with non-attention to perceptions of variety,[15] thinking: 'Space is infinite,' some monk enters upon and abides in the sphere of infinite space; and he then might think: 'I am abiding in effacement.' But in the Noble One's discipline it is not these (attainments) that are called 'effacement'; in the Noble One's discipline they are called 'peaceful abidings.'

9. "It may be that by entirely transcending the sphere of infinite space, thinking: 'Consciousness is infinite,' some monk enters and abides in the sphere of infinite consciousness; and he then might think: 'I am abiding in effacement.' But in the Noble One's discipline it is not these (attainments) that are called 'effacement'; in the Noble One's discipline they are called 'peaceful abidings.'

10. "It may be that by entirely transcending the sphere of infinite consciousness, some monk enters and abides in the sphere of nothingness; and he then might think: 'I am abiding in effacement.' But in the Noble One's discipline it is not these (attainments) that are called 'effacement'; in the Noble One's discipline they are called 'peaceful abidings.'

11. "It may be that, by entirely transcending the sphere of nothingness, some monk enters and abides in

the sphere of neither-perception-nor-non-perception; and he then might think: 'I am abiding in effacement.' But in the Noble One's discipline it is not these (attainments) that are called 'effacement'; in the Noble One's discipline they are called 'peaceful abidings.'

Effacement

12. "But herein, Cunda, effacement should be practised by you:[16]

(1) Others will be harmful; we shall not be harmful here—thus effacement can be done.[17]

(2) Others will kill living beings; we shall abstain from killing living beings here—thus effacement can be done.

(3) Others will take what is not given; we shall abstain from taking what is not given here—thus effacement can be done.

(4) Others will be unchaste; we shall be chaste here—thus effacement can be done.

(5) Others will speak falsehood; we shall abstain from false speech here—thus effacement can be done.

(6) Others will speak maliciously; we shall abstain from malicious speech here—thus effacement can be done.

(7) Others will speak harshly; we shall abstain from harsh speech here—thus effacement can be done.

(8) Others will gossip; we shall abstain from gossip here—thus effacement can be done.

(9) Others will be covetous; we shall not be covetous here—thus effacement can be done.

(10) Others will have thoughts of ill will; we shall not have thoughts of ill will here—thus effacement can be done.

(11) Others will have wrong views; we shall have right view here—thus effacement can be done.

(12) Others will have wrong intention; we shall have right intention here—thus effacement can be done.

(13) Others will use wrong speech; we shall use right speech here—thus effacement can be done.

(14) Others will commit wrong actions; we shall do right actions here—thus effacement can be done.

(15) Others will have wrong livelihood; we shall have right livelihood here—thus effacement can be done.

(16) Others will make wrong effort; we shall make right effort here—thus effacement can be done.

(17) Others will have wrong mindfulness; we shall have right mindfulness here—thus effacement can be done.

(18) Others will have wrong concentration; we shall have right concentration here—thus effacement can be done.

(19) Others will have wrong knowledge; we shall have right knowledge here—thus effacement can be done.

(20) Others will have wrong deliverance; we shall have right deliverance here—thus effacement can be done.

(21) Others will be overcome by sloth and torpor; we shall be free from sloth and torpor here—thus effacement can be done.

(22) Others will be agitated; we shall be unagitated here—thus effacement can be done.

(23) Others will be doubting; we shall be free from doubt here—thus effacement can be done.

(24) Others will be angry; we shall not be angry here—thus effacement can be done.

(25) Others will be hostile; we shall not be hostile here—thus effacement can be done.

(26) Others will denigrate; we shall not denigrate here—thus effacement can be done.

(27) Others will be domineering; we shall not be domineering here—thus effacement can be done.

(28) Others will be envious; we shall not be envious here—thus effacement can be done.

(29) Others will be jealous; we shall not be jealous here—thus effacement can be done.

(30) Others will be fraudulent; we shall not be fraudulent here—thus effacement can be done.

(31) Others will be hypocrites; we shall not be hypocrites here—thus effacement can be done.

(32) Others will be obstinate; we shall not be obstinate here—thus effacement can be done.

(33) Others will be arrogant; we shall not be arrogant here—thus effacement can be done.

(34) Others will be difficult to admonish; we shall be easy to admonish here—thus effacement can be done.

(35) Others will have bad friends; we shall have noble friends here—thus effacement can be done.

(36) Others will be negligent; we shall be heedful here—thus effacement can be done.

(37) Others will be faithless; we shall be faithful here—thus effacement can be done.

(38) Others will be shameless; we shall be shameful here—thus effacement can be done.

(39) Others will be without conscience; we shall have conscience here—thus effacement can be done.

(40) Others will have no learning; we shall be learned here—thus effacement can be done.

(41) Others will be idle; we shall be energetic here—thus effacement can be done.

(42) Others will be lacking in mindfulness; we shall be established in mindfulness here—thus effacement can be done.

(43) Others will be without wisdom; we shall be endowed with wisdom—thus effacement can be done.

(44) Others will misapprehend according to their individual views, hold on to them tenaciously and not easily discard them;[18] we shall not misapprehend according to individual views nor hold on to them tenaciously, but shall discard them with ease—thus effacement can be done.

The Arising of Thought

13. "Cunda, I say that even the arising of a thought concerned with salutary things (and ideas)[19] is of great importance, not to speak of bodily acts and words conforming (to such thought).[20] Therefore, Cunda:

(1) The thought should be produced: 'Others will be harmful; we shall not be harmful here.'

(2) The thought should be produced: 'Others will kill living beings; we shall abstain from killing living beings here.'

(3)-(43) . . .

(44) The thought should be produced: 'Others will misapprehend according to their individual views, hold on to them tenaciously and not easily discard them; we shall not misapprehend according to individual views nor hold on to them tenaciously, but shall discard them with ease.'

Avoidance

14. "Suppose, Cunda, there were an an uneven road and another even road by which to avoid it; and suppose there were an uneven ford and another even ford by which to avoid it.[21] So too:

(1) A person given to harmfulness has non-harming by which to avoid it.

(2) A person given to killing living beings has abstention from killing by which to avoid it.

(3) A person given to taking what is not given has abstention from taking what is not given by which to avoid it.

(4) A person given to unchastity has chastity by which to avoid it.

(5) A person given to false speech has abstention from false speech by which to avoid it.

(6) A person given to malicious speech has abstention from malicious speech by which to avoid it.

(7) A person given to harsh speech has abstention from harsh speech by which to avoid it.

(8) A person given to gossip has abstention from gossip by which to avoid it.

(9) A person given to covetousness has non-covetousness by which to avoid it.

(10) A person given to thoughts of ill will has non-ill will by which to avoid it.

(11) A person given to wrong view has right view by which to avoid it.

(12) A person given to wrong intention has right intention by which to avoid it.

(13) A person given to wrong speech has right speech by which to avoid it.

(14) A person given to wrong action has right action by which to avoid it.

(15) A person given to wrong livelihood has right livelihood by which to avoid it.

(16) A person given to wrong effort has right effort by which to avoid it.

(17) A person given to wrong mindfulness has right mindfulness by which to avoid it.

(18) A person given to wrong concentration has right concentration by which to avoid it.

(19) A person given to wrong knowledge has right knowledge by which to avoid it.

(20) A person given to wrong deliverance has right deliverance by which to avoid it.

(21) A person overcome by sloth and torpor has freedom from sloth and torpor by which to avoid it.

(22) A person given to agitation has non-agitation by which to avoid it.

(23) A person given to doubting has freedom from doubt by which to avoid it.

(24) A person given to anger has freedom from anger by which to avoid it.

(25) A person given to hostility has freedom from hostility by which to avoid it.

(26) A person given to denigrating has non-denigrating by which to avoid it.

(27) A person given to domineering has non-domineering by which to avoid it.

(28) A person given to envy has non-envy by which to avoid it.

(29) A person given to jealousy has non-jealousy by which to avoid it.

(30) A person given to fraud has non-fraud by which to avoid it.

(31) A person given to hypocrisy has non-hypocrisy by which to avoid it.

(32) A person given to obstinacy has non-obstinacy by which to avoid it.

(33) A person given to arrogance has non-arrogance by which to avoid it.

(34) A person difficult to admonish has amenability by which to avoid it.

(35) A person given to making bad friends has making good friends by which to avoid it.

(36) A person given to negligence has heedfulness by which to avoid it.

(37) A person given to faithlessness has faith by which to avoid it.

(38) A person given to shamelessness has shame by which to avoid it.

(39) A person without conscience has conscience by which to avoid it.

(40) A person without learning has acquisition of great learning by which to avoid it.

(41) A person given to idleness has energetic endeavour by which to avoid it.

(42) A person without mindfulness has the establishment of mindfulness by which to avoid it.

(43) A person without wisdom has wisdom by which to avoid it.

(44) A person given to misapprehending according to his individual views, to holding on to them tenaciously and not discarding them easily, has non-misapprehension of individual views, non-holding on tenaciously and ease in discarding by which to avoid it.

The Way Upward

15. "Cunda, as all unsalutary states lead downward and all salutary states lead upward, even so, Cunda:

(1) A person given to harmfulness has harmlessness to lead him upward.[22]

(2) A person given to killing living beings has abstention from killing to lead him upwards.

(3)-(43) . . .

(44) A person given to misapprehending according to his individual views, to holding on to them tenaciously and not discarding them easily, has non-misapprehension of individual views, non-holding on tenaciously and ease in discarding to lead him upward.

Quenching

16. "Cunda, it is impossible that one who is himself sunk in the mire[23] should pull out another who is sunk in the mire. But it is possible, Cunda, that one not sunk in the mire himself should pull out another who is sunk in the mire.

"It is not possible, Cunda, that one who is himself not restrained, not disciplined and not quenched (as to his passions),[24] should make others restrained and disciplined, should make them attain to the full quenching (of passions).[25] But it is possible, Cunda, that one who is himself restrained, disciplined and fully quenched (as to his passions) should make others restrained and disciplined, should make them attain to the full quenching (of passions). Even so, Cunda:[26]

(1) A person given to harmfulness has harmlessness by which to attain to the full quenching (of it).

(2) A person given to killing living beings has abstention from killing by which to attain to the full quenching (of it).

(3)-(43) . . .

(44) A person given to misapprehending according to his individual views, to holding on to them tenaciously and not discarding them easily, has non-misapprehension of individual views, non-holding on tenaciously and ease in discarding by which to attain the quenching (of them).

Conclusion

17. "Thus, Cunda, I have shown to you the instruction on effacement, I have shown to you the instruction on thought's arising, I have shown to you the instruction on avoidance, I have shown to you the instruction on the way upward, I have shown to you the instruction on quenching.

18. "What can be done for his disciples by a Master who seeks their welfare and has compassion and pity on them, that I have done for you, Cunda.[27] There are these roots of trees, there are empty places. Meditate, Cunda, do not delay, lest you later regret it. This is my message to you."

Thus spoke the Blessed One. Satisfied, the venerable Cunda rejoiced in the Blessed One's words.

* * *

The concluding verse added by the Theras of the First Council:

> Deep like the ocean is this Suttanta on Effacement,
> Dealing with forty-four items, showing them in five sections.

Notes

1. Mahā-Cunda Thera was the brother of the venerable Sāriputta Thera.

2. *Self-doctrines or world-doctrines (atta-vāda, lokavāda).* According to Comy., this refers: (a) to the twenty types of personality-belief *(sakkāya-diṭṭhi),* i. e. four for each of the five aggregates *(khandha);* (b) to eight wrong views about self and world, as being eternal, not eternal, both eternal and not eternal, neither eternal nor not eternal, and the same four alternatives concerning finite and infinite.

3. *In a monk who is only at the beginning of his (meditative) reflections (ādim-eva manasikaroto).* Comy.: "This refers to one who is at the beginning of his insight-meditation *(vipassanā-bhāvanā)* and has not yet attained to Stream-entry," when the fetter of personality-belief is finally eliminated. The beginner's insight-practice extends from the "discernment of mentality and corporeality" *(nāmarūpa-pariccheda)* up to the "knowledge of rise and fall" *(udayabbaya-ñāṇa),* on which see *Path of Purification (Visuddhimagga),* Chs. XVIII, XX, XXI.

According to the Comy., the Thera's question concerns those who overrate the degree of their achievement, i. e. those who believe that, in their meditative practice, they have achieved this or that result while actually they have not. Overestimation *(abhimāna),* in that sense, "does not arise in ignorant common people *(bāla-puthujjana)* who are entirely engrossed in worldly life, nor does it arise in Noble

Disciples *(ariya-sāvaka)*; because in a Stream-winner the overestimation does not arise that he is a Once-returner, etc. Self-overestimation can occur only in one who actually practises (meditation) and has temporarily subdued the defilements by way of tranquillity or insight. Mahā-Cunda Thera, being an Arahat, was no self-overrater himself, but in formulating his question, he put himself in the place of one who is; or, as others say, there may have been such "self-overraters" among his pupils, and for conveying to them the Buddha's reply, he put his question.

4. *(The object) in which (yattha).* Comy.: *yattha* (where) = *yasmiṁ ārammaṇe*. The object, or basis, are the five aggregates, because all false views on self and world can refer only to the five aggregates or to one of them. See *Discourse on the Snake Simile* (Wheel No. 47/48), p. 8, and *Anattā and Nibbāna*, by Nyanaponika Thera (Wheel No. 11), p. 18 (quotation).

5. *In which these views arise (yattha uppajjanti)*, i. e. arise for the first time, without having occurred earlier (Comy.).

Underlie (anusenti), i. e. habitually occur (cf. *anusaya*, "tendency," which may be latent or active). Comy.: "This refers to views which, having been indulged in repeatedly, have become strong and have not been removed." Sub.Comy.: "By ultimate elimination *(samuccheda-vinaya-vasena)*."

Become active (samudācaranti). Comy.: "Wrong views that have arrived at the (action-) doors of body and speech," i. e. which have found expression in words and deeds.

6. *With right wisdom (sammappaññāya).* Comy.: "With insight-wisdom, ending with the knowledge pertaining to the path of Stream-entry."

7. *As it actually is (yathā-bhūtaṁ).* Comy.: "Because the five aggregates exist only in that manner (i. e. as something 'that is not mine,' etc.). But if conceived in the way 'It is mine,' etc., it simply does not exist *(n'ev'atthi).*"

8. *This is not mine:* hereby craving *(taṇhā)* is rejected.

9. *This I am not:* this refers to the rejection of conceit *(māna).*

10. *This is not my self:* this refers to the rejection of false views *(diṭṭhi).*

11. *Abandoning . . . discarding (pahānaṁ . . . paṭinissaggo).* Comy.: "Both terms are synonymous with the ultimate eradication of wrong views, taking place at Stream-entry when the fetter of personality belief is destroyed."

12. Now the Buddha speaks, on his own, of another type of "self-overrater," i. e. of those who have realized any of the eight meditative attainments *(samāpatti)* and believe that this signifies true "effacement" *(sallekha).*

The common meaning of *sallekha** is austere prac-

---

* *Sallekha* (= *sam-lekha*) is derived from the verbal root *likh*, to scratch; hence *likhati* (a) to scratch in, to write; (b) to scratch off, to remove: *sam-likhati,* "to remove fully." An interesting parallel

tice or asceticism; but in the Buddha's usage it is the radical "effacing" or removal of the defilements.

The eight stages of meditation given here in the discourse, consist of the four fine-material absorptions *(rūpajjhāna)* and the four immaterial absorptions *(arūpajjhāna)*. Comy. says that these meditative attainments "are in common with the ascetics outside (the Buddha's Dispensation)."

Comy.: "The overrater's meditative absorption is neither 'effacement' nor is it the 'path of practice for effacement' *(sallekha-paṭipadā)*. And why not? Because that jhāna is not used by him as a basis for insight; that is, after rising from jhāna he does not scrutinise the (physical and mental) formations" (see *Visuddhimagga* transl. by Ñāṇamoli, Ch. XVIII, 3). His jhāna produces only one-pointedness of mind, and is, as our text says, an "abiding in ease here and now."

13. "By *'perceptions of corporeality'* *(rūpasaññā)* are meant the absorptions of the fine-material sphere *(rūpajjhāna)* as well as those things that are their objects" (*Visuddhimagga*).

14. *Perceptions of sense-response* (lit. resistance, *paṭigha-saññā*) are perceptions arisen through the impact of the physical sense bases (eye, etc.) and their objects.

---

is "ascesis," derived from the Greek *askeuein*, to scratch. The rendering by "effacement" is Ñāṇamoli Thera's; Soma Thera has "cancelling"; I. B. Horner, "expunging."

15. *Perceptions of variety (nānatta-saññā)* are perceptions that arise in a variety of fields, or various perceptions in various fields. This refers to all perceptions belonging to the sense sphere *(kāmāvacara)*.

16. Comy.: "Now, the Blessed One shows in forty-four ways where effacement should be practised. But why are harmlessness and the other states regarded as effacement, unlike the eight meditative attainments? Because they are a basis for the supramundane *(lokuttara-pādaka)*; while, for outsiders, the eight attainments are merely a basis for (continuing) the round of existence *(vaṭṭa-pādaka)*, (because by non-Buddhists they are practised for the sake of rebirth in higher worlds). But in the Buddha's Dispensation, even the Going for Refuge is a basis for the supramundane.

Sub.Comy.: "If one, wishing to overcome the suffering of saṁsāra, goes with joyful confidence for refuge to the Triple Gem, then this Refuge will be for him a supporting condition for higher virtue, etc. (i. e. higher mentality and higher wisdom), and it may gradually lead him to the attainment of the path of understanding *(dassana-magga*; i. e. Stream-entry)."

The Forty-four Ways of Effacement

(1) *Harmful* and *harmless* are not attached to a group of standard doctrinal categories as most of the other qualities are. On "harmlessness" see Note 17.

(2)-(11) are the courses of action (*kammapatha*), unsalutary (*akusala*) and salutary (*kusala*), referring to body (2-4), speech (5-8) and mind (9-11).

(12)-(18) are the last seven factors of the eightfold path (wrong and right), also called the eight states of wrongness or rightness (*micchatta, sammatta*). The first path factor, right (or wrong) view, is not separately mentioned, being identical with (11).

(19)-(20) are often added to the eightfold path.

(21)-(23) are the last three of the five hindrances (*nīvaraṇa*); the first two are identical with (9) and (10), and therefore not repeated here.

(24)-(33) are ten of the sixteen defilements (*upakkilesa*) mentioned in M. 7 (Simile of the Cloth).

(34)-(36) are called in the Commentary the miscellaneous factors (*pakiṇṇaka*).

(37)-(43) are the seven "good qualities" (*saddhammā*), mentioned in M. 53. Comy.: "In this connection they are mentioned as forming the complete equipment required for insight (*vipassanā-sambhāro paripūro*)."

(44) is unattached to any group of terms. (See Note 18).

17. Comy.: "Harmlessness is called 'effacement,' because it effaces harmfulness, i. e. it cuts it off (*chindati*). This method of explanation applies to all other terms."

Sub.Comy.: "But why is harmlessness (or non-violence, *ahiṁsā*) mentioned at the very beginning? Because it is the root of all virtues; harmlessness, namely, is a synonym of compassion. Especially, it is the root-cause of morality because it makes one refrain from immorality which has as its characteristic mark the harming of others. Just as the killing of living beings has the harming of others as its mark, so also the taking away of others' property; for 'robbing a man's wealth is worse than stabbing him.'* Similarly, chastity removes the cause for the pains of child bearing, etc., and there is hardly a need to mention the harm done by adultery.

"Obvious is also the harm done to others by deception, by causing dissension and by backbiting. The mark of harming others is also attached to gossip because it takes away what is beneficial and causes to arise what is not beneficial; to covetousness, as it causes one to take what is not given; to ill will, as it causes killing, etc.; to wrong views, as they are the cause of all that is unbeneficial. One who holds wrong views may, in the conviction of acting righteously, kill living beings and incite others to do likewise. There is nothing to say about other (and lesser immoral acts induced by false views).

"Harmlessness (i. e. the principle of non-violence) has the characteristic mark of making one refrain from immorality which, on its part, has the mark of harming. Hence harmlessness is an especially strong

---

* This is given in Pali as direct speech or quote; perhaps it was a common adage.

productive cause of morality; and morality, again, is the basis for concentration of mind, while concentration is the basis for wisdom. In that way harmlessness (non-violence) is the root of all virtues.

"Furthermore, in the case of the highest type of men *(uttamapurisa)* who have noble aspirations, who act considerately and wisely, also their mental concentration and their wisdom, just as their morality, is conducive to the weal and happiness of others. In that way, too, compassion is the root of all virtues, and therefore it has been mentioned at the beginning.

"Now, (after harmlessness), the salutary courses of action *(kusala-kammapatha*; 2-11) are included to show that these states are produced by harmlessness. Then follow the eight states of rightness (11-18) to show that they must be brought about by basing them on morality, which is the root of these virtues. Now the separation from the hindrances (21-23, and 16, 17) is included to indicate that this is the primary task for one intent on purifying (his practice of) the eightfold path. Then follows the cleansing from the defilements (24-33) to indicate that effacement is accomplished by giving up anger (24), etc. And the cleansing from the defilements will be successful when aided by amenability to advice, noble friendship and heedful diligence (34-36).

"Now the seven noble qualities (37-43) are included to show that they will come to perfection in him who is endowed with amenability and the other (two factors); and that they, on their part, after having strengthened insight, will lead to the paths of sanctitude. (See end of Note 16.)

"Finally, the passage on 'misapprehending according to one's individual views,' etc., (44) is meant to indicate that for such a one (i. e. for one bent on effacement) that wrong attitude is an obstacle to the attainment of the supramundane virtues and is, therefore, to be avoided totally. This passage on misapprehending (about which see Note 18) is also meant to show that one who, by the right conduct here described, is in the process of attaining one of the paths of sanctitude, will be led to the acme of effacement (by this last-mentioned threefold way of effacement).

"In this manner should be understood the purpose of stating these forty-four modes of effacement as well as the order in which they appear in the discourse."

18. Comy.: "A single wrong view (or wrong attitude), which is an obstacle for the supramundane qualities and hence does not lead to emancipation, is here described in three aspects:

(a) *Others will misapprehend according to their individual views (sandiṭṭhi-parāmāsī)*. Sub.Comy.: *sa(m) = attano*, one's own. *Parāmāsī* means setting aside the actual nature of a thing, one conceives it differently *(sabhāvaṁ atikkamitvā parato āmasana)*.

(b) *Hold on tenaciously (ādhānaggāhī)*. Sub. Comy.: *ādhāna = daḷha*, tight, firm.

(c) *Discards not easily*. Comy.: "There are those who can discard their views on seeing a convincing reason. But others, even if shown many reasons, cannot give up their views; and of them it is said that they 'do not discard easily.' It refers to those who cling firmly to a subjective view that has occurred to them, believing 'only this is the truth.' Even if the Buddhas or others show them reasons, they do not relinquish their views. Such people, whatever idea they conceive, be it in accordance with Dhamma or not, will say: 'So it has been told by our teacher. So we have learned it'; and they will withdraw into themselves like a turtle drawing its limbs into its shell. They hold on to their views with the tight grip of a crocodile and do not let go."

19. *Salutary: kusala*, also translated by wholesome, profitable, skilful. These salutary things, says Sub. Comy., are the modes of effacement mentioned.

20. Sub.Comy.: "For those who cannot take up, by actual application, the practice of effacement, even the arising of a thought *(cittuppādo)*, i. e. an inclination for it, is of great importance.

Comy. says that a salutary thought is of great importance as it leads entirely to weal and happiness, and as it is the cause for the subsequent actions conforming to it. Examples are given beginning with the intention to give almsfood to monks, up to the aspiration for Buddhahood. The Sub.Comy., however, says that in some cases the importance is not in the thought itself but only in the actual execution of it. This certainly applies to the intention to give alms, etc. But in the efforts for effacing the defilements, the formation of a mental attitude directed towards it, in other words, the heart's resolve, is certainly an important factor.

This section of the discourse has been condensed in the present translation. But he who has chosen the path of effacement as his way of practice *(paṭipadā)* is well advised to repeat all forty-four items, linking them with his heart's earnest resolve. Also, the last two sections of the discourse have been condensed.

21. Comy.: "*Parikkamana* (lit. going around, circumventing) has the meaning of 'avoiding' *(parivajjana)*. For the avoiding of harmfulness there is the ready road of harmlessness, walking on which one may easily experience felicity among humans or deities, or one may cross over (by that ford) from this world (to the other shore, Nibbāna). The same method of explanation applies to the other sentences."

22. Comy.: "The meaning is this: Any unsalutary states of mind, whether they produce rebirth or not, and whether, in a given rebirth, they produce kamma results or not—all, because of their type, i. e. by being unsalutary, lead downwards (to lower worlds). They are just like that because, on the occasion of their yielding a kamma result, that result will be undesirable and unpleasant.

"Any salutary states of mind, whether they produce rebirth or not, and whether, in a given rebirth, they produce kamma results or not—all, because of their type, lead upwards. They are just like that because, on the occasion of their yielding a kamma result, that result will be desirable and pleasant.

"The connection (in the discourse, between the general principle stated first, and its specific application to the forty-four cases) is as follows: Just as unsalutary states lead downwards, so it is with that one state of harmfulness for him who is harmful. Just as all salutary states lead upwards, so it is with that one state of harmlessness for him who is harmless."

23. Comy.: "In the Noble One's discipline, the 'mire' is a name for the five sense desires."

24. *Not fully quenched (aparinibbuto)*. Comy.: "with defilements not extinguished *(anibbuta-kilesa)*."

25. Comy.: "There may be those who object that this is not correct because some come to penetration of the Dhamma *(dhammābhisamaya*, i. e. Stream-entry) after listening to an exposition of the Teaching by monks or nuns, male or female lay followers, who are still worldlings *(puthujjana*; i. e. have not attained to any of the paths of sanctitude). Hence one who is still in the mire *can* pull out others. (Reply:) This should not be understood in that way. It is the Blessed One who here does the pulling out.

"Suppose there is a king who sends a letter to the border region, and the people there, unable to read it by themselves, have the letter read to them by another able to do it. Having learned of the contents, they respond with respect, knowing it as the king's order. But they do not think that it is the letter reader's order; he will receive praise only for his smooth and fluent reading of the letter. Similarly, even if preachers of the ability of Sāriputta Thera expound the Dhamma, still they are just like readers of a letter written by another. Their sermon should truly be attributed to the Blessed One, like the decree to the king. The preachers, however, receive their limited praise, just because they expound the Dhamma with a smooth and fluent diction. Hence that statement in the discourse is correct."

26. For the connection between the modes of effacement and the preceding simile, Comy. gives two alternative explanations:

(a) Just as one who is not sunk in the mire himself can pull others out of it, similarly he who is harmless himself can quench another's harmful volition.

(b) Just as only he who has quenched his own passions can help one who has not quenched them, similarly only a volition of harmlessness can quench a harmful volition.

27. Comy.: "So far goes a compassionate teacher's task, namely, the correct exposition of his teaching; beyond that, namely, the practice (according to the teaching; *paṭipatti*), is the task of the disciples."